salmonpoetry

Diverse Voices from Ireland and the World

the arts council
an chomhairle ealaíon

funding
literature
artscouncil.ie

Love in the Original Language

Poems by
Fióna Bolger

Katherine
Hope you enjoy this

Love n hys
fiona

Published in 2022 by
Salmon Poetry
Cliffs of Moher, County Clare, Ireland
Website: www.salmonpoetry.com
Email: info@salmonpoetry.com

ISBN 978-1-915022-16-5

Cover & Title Page Image:
Joby Hickey – www.jobyhickey.com

Cover Design & Typesetting: *Siobhán Hutson*

Printed in Ireland by Sprint Print

*Salmon Poetry gratefully acknowledges the support of
The Arts Council / An Chomhairle Ealaíon*

Justice is what love looks like in public.

—CORNEL WEST

...talking love, talking revolution
which is love spelled backwards...

—DIANE DI PRIMA

*My family of bone, blood, food and words, here, there and everywhere,
it is you who have taught me love in all of your languages
in your original ways. Without you, none of this.*

Contents

A Linkister Plays with Quantum Reality

We are doing lob-pidgin,
lobbing our words back
and forth. You ishq mine
and I pyaar yours. Back
and forth we lob these loves.
Each time they fly back

and forth, they exist in me
and you. I cannot hold
all the words in my head
or even all of one word.
Right now, a little piece of this
exists inside your head.

The End of October

What we feel is beyond words:
We should be ashamed of our poems.

        Nizar Qabbani

i

men pierce rubber craft
waves lay bodies on the sand

ii

'You have to understand our mentality.
We are seafaring people. We know
what it means when a person's
in danger. They have to be taken
to safety. A dead body has to be recovered
given back to the family.'

iii

níl aon tinteán
mar do thinteán féin

iv

'facing the damp hungry cold
between borders we wish
we could go home'

v

'There was an attachment to things.
So long as you had your wardrobe,
your handbags, if you had your bed linen,
life was bearable.'

vi

It is safer to live under terror, where your soul
is tethered, than risk bombings daily.

vii

…and Rabbit started a campaign
against Kanga and Roo, until the other
creatures told him to shut up.

viii

Anyone can see that no matter how small or how
distant a person is a person wherever they are.

ix

How quickly we dismember the past and remember
history in a new and improved formula.

x

Coffin ships
Diseased Irish
Ellis Island

xi

'My grieved country,
In a flash
You changed me from a poet who wrote love poems
To a poet who writes with a knife.'

xii

These are the days of the dead
the living are silenced
by the deafening emptiness.

Ranger Dominance

Woken from short sleep
before dawn, drowsy
time for knock and searches
compulsory co-operation

Didn't know what to say
so I said
Roger that Sir!

Waking women
invading homes
rooftop snipers aim: neck, thigh
under threat, return fire

Didn't know what to say
so I said
Roger that Sir!

We hear an Apache cannon
in the distance—go see
engaging eight men, armed
with a telephoto lens

Didn't know what to say
so I said
Roger that Sir!

Shit, piss, blood in the heat
the stink of fear and death
the sound of crying
Let's get out of here

Didn't know what to say
so I said
Roger that Sir!

Child's face studded with glass
I pick her up, my daughter
the boy, did he move?
Quit being a pussy

Didn't know what to say
so I said
Roger that Sir!

Their blood stains my uniform
I try to clean it
You could be charged
with malingering

Didn't know what to say
so I said
Roger that Sir!

Numbers

i.m. Yussef Mohamed (died aged 11, Aleppo)

we've stopped counting the bodies
the doctor said at the start

but now the medics can be counted
on one hand

and children whose ages are barely
double-digit, are nursing the injured

Yussef cannot count the times
he pumps air into the child's lungs

he doesn't mention
the number of bodies he sees

but the scattered body parts
he remembers

Ghazal for Parveena and her son, Javaid

(disappeared 1991)

Where have you hidden my new crescent moon?
I search for my son by the light of the moon

A hawk swooped down and took him away
is he high in the mountains, near to the moon?

When he disappeared my fear went away
I approach the armed men under sun and moon.

I've searched camps, hospitals and jails
where is he? Can my child see the moon?

I watched over my son as he grew
under the waxing and waning of the moon.

The bodies they've found prove our worst fears
the tears of the living light up the moon.

I cannot forget his bright sunny face
grey corpses glitter beneath the full moon.

Stranded at Sea

we are alone
I radio from the ship
we've no-one to help us

we have packed clothes
paid gunmen and fled
we are alone

we are far from home
crossed border and border
we've no-one to help us

gave our savings at the port
everything precious is gone
we are alone

we hope this boat road
leads to safe land
we've no-one to help us

the law is silent
this far out to sea
we are alone
we've no-one to help us

No Child is Born to Flicker in the Shadows

I open my daughter's new Irish passport
and printed beneath the mountains
rivers and coast line, I find

It is the entitlement and birthright
of every person born in the island
of Ireland which includes its islands and seas
to be part of the Irish nation.

for one crazy moment
I believe this is true

Translated from a Libyan Life in Ireland

i   mojewdia

the room is cold
the rising light cuts
through my sleep
I boil the kettle
make coffee black enough
to dissolve my memories

daytime I sit in Bewleys
drink sweetness with women
of uncertain age
talk politics read papers

evening finds me at the bar in Whelan's
with out-of-training newshounds
busy lapping pints
yapping as the news flickers by

most nights I like to dance
I swing samba salsa
movement under cover of darkness
my natural element

and in dead of night
I'm woken by the distant past
I turn on the radio
the crackle distorts the silence

I had heard others die
a blow-by-blow account
but when my sister died
there was no transmission
not a whisper did I hear of her

ii waheed

maybe it was prison life
but I could not sleep alone
the American did not understand
she raged, raided my room
shredded my clothes
left me bare

the girl I wanted too
but she was young
too young to bother
when I cheated
laughed it off
and walked away

and I was left alone
to cook for one
alone with the world news
the nights were long
and dark—stretching

iii Umm Taufiq

I have your face
here in my hands
my tribal markings
deeper invisible
ley lines in my soul
I've destroyed my papers
letters, lovers' photos
many times, but yours
I've treasured, ya ma ma
my departure shamed you
come to me now that I may
give you a hero's welcome
salamaat salamaat salamaat

iv fatwa

I buy that book
I have not read Quran
in many years
but if this man
is under threat of death
for speech
and I have suffered
for my belief
I want to see
to understand

the words are like prods
nerves long numb
communicate pain to me
organs I have lived without
begin to quiver
cleanse my blood
remove the toxins
from my brain

I clearly see the man's mistake
these people I had
sided with against my own
they will not mock
their holy books
but mine, they'll tear apart
and I am torn apart

v   al Ummah

pulled too thin
I became see-through
their embrace
made me solid
matter once more

under cover of her darkness
I found a quiet place
to settle myself
return to childhood
unbroken sleep

Hunter's Moon, Belfast 2016

They sing *The Men Behind the Wire*
and we are all behind the cage,
inside the Sunflower pub.
He recalls the blackened smell of soldiers
out to raid the homes of children
made fearful in their beds.

In another pub they call you 'mate'.
The squaddies speak of Andiestown, and you
must swallow your perspective, flatten yourself
to fit the space they've kept for you.

You have held a loaded tongue
kept silence when words would only
wound and tried to find another way
to spell across a no-man's land.

Cryptolect

is a way to smuggle meaning between people,
past borders of misunderstanding. Speakers slip
their tongues between syllables, shift the sounds
in their mouths, mixing them up just enough

to confuse the non-speaker, outsider.
There's a challenge to learning what is hidden,
the thrill of knowledge not found in books.
If you are there, if it's spoken before you, if you listen,

you will learn, if they trust you. In the crypt of the lect
lie the remains of those whose words were understood,
who did not manage to dodge between dialects. Forbidden
words of desire, hidden words of escape, codes to keep you alive,

some become slang to an outside world, while others
remain a secret chant of belonging, spelling safety and love.

Ossuary

Dig
down into the bones of the matter.
I am searching for a way to embody borders,
to absorb the body of borders, to border the body,
to be a body crossing borders, to break through
borders, transgress, translate myself from this side
to that, from this meaning to that and yet be
on both sides, or between, be.

Skin
is the border of the body, but the territory of me
is bone and sinew and flesh, organs which play music
which keep me alive and when they cascade I die.

Blood
poisoning: a small infection crosses my skin border
moves, multiplies, attacks my organs, dissonance,
interference and I am left rotting from inside out. A gut full
of bacteria ready to take over when I am down
and left out on the soil, from inside and out, I become soil.

Words
encoded in our breath, a gift to those who feel the warmth
of that breath. The past and future of the word, not necessary.
It is in my breath now. I blow meaning to you and you absorb
it into the depth of your ear. Once lungbound, now the sound
of me is inside you. That is communication. That is connection.
We hear with our bones and the water of our ears.

Cryptolect
a way to smuggle meaning between people, past borders
of misunderstanding. A language ceases to be a cryptolect
when it is more widely known.

Bone
deep bodyache of long hours of travel, of too cold
and too hot absorbed into clothes, the nerve tremble
of standing in line, when you might be pulled out,
might be further questioned, want to scream out
to end the waiting, but don't, hoping that you
will make it through, that they'll believe you
or ignore you as they are ignoring now. You
do not exist in all these hours before
and if you get through you will cease to exist
again. That moment when you are alone
before the officer, before the camera,
the computer screen saying you don't know what,
hope it is bland, unexceptional.

Sitting
you see them to the sides of this standing crowd
the chosen, chosen to wait, chosen to be further questioned,
chosen without being given a choice. You know the feeling
of sitting out, not knowing what's next. Hoping it will be over,
they'll say bye and let you by.

Profile
is it her name
is it your clothes
is it random
is it
is it
is it

Sound
of bones, the sound of bamboos knocking in the forest wind,
an organ playing for all to hear. Would the bones of the famine
victims, who died after the flowering of bamboo, after the rat
population explosion, after the grain was eaten by those rodents,
would those people, would their bones, would my bones, your bones
sound like bamboo? Would there be a tune and who will hear our bone
song?

Vultures
eat me, drop dead flesh on balconies as I lie naked
in the Tower of Silence, borrowing space
from a people who know in their bones their texts
were burned in Alexandria. There is no book to bang
only the gentle breath of word from generation
to generation, from lungbound to ear bone.

(Im)mobile
For all our technology we are skin and bone. Our borders built
from the wattle and daub of migrant bones and dried skin, caked
with the mud of transit countries, the dessicated words of asylum
protection and human rights. Their meaning gnawed away, marrow
sucked out by the powerful. In other places the border is sodden
clothes, sleeping bags, tents, odd shoes, single socks, flotation
devices of all kinds in bright colours, useful as children's toys.
The detritus makes up the line of demarcation, dehumanisation,
the mark of decimation.

Border
I want to embody,
show on my body,
display the dead bodies
of my family,
my people.
Here let us wake them,
wake them and answer
them for why they have
died.

Mohn and Memory

after Paul Celan

These are the days of moan and memory. They last longer than a
thousand nights. We speak darkness around us, wrap ourselves in
forgetting because this is the hour of weariness, a time to silence
ourselves and let go secrets. In this nightmare, we sleep awake.

Repose brings only disquiet. It is time.
Let us do the work of remembering, recovering, recording. Es ist Zeit.
Let us memorise the past by degrees. It is time.
Mohn and memory, music without silence is meaningless,
memory without forgetting is cacophony. Es ist Zeit.
The blankness on the page, the space between words,
the meaning that skips zwischen Sprachen. It is time.

Is memory longer than history?
Is history longer than the present?
Is the present longer than us?

When the day lasts longer than a thousand nights, then you speak
yourself, you silence yourself, you light yourself, you darken
yourself. Each moment pearl layered.

Sadness solidified and hidden, the silence between. Es ist Zeit.

Natural History

the dead whale bones
hang preserved in the museum
I look up to see their length and breadth
I long to touch the smoothness
feel the still warmth
but cannot reach

only my voice carries
up and up my song goes
the melody wrapping itself
around the skeleton
until fully fleshed
the massive mammal
flails mid-air
longing for her native element

the struggle to survive
fills the gallery with broken glass
stuffed animals strewn about
dismembered, bloodless
memories of murder

calmer now
suspended in a hammock
by so many straining seagulls
winging towards the Grand Canal
the whale is gently lowered
hitting the water happily
submerging herself

rising again to navigate
the locks reach river Liffey
then open sea
and learn to sing again
deep and echoing

Canal Bank Sonnet

The sun clears away the frost of sleep
from grass wearing its winter look.
Black-hoods walk the towpath pulling
barges of contracts, agreements,

accounts and bills. Hard hats eat up
the city, building by building. Brick
after brick ground to dust
in their mechanical mandibles

devouring soft human tents
and warm sleeping bags. Dust
clings to nearby windows.
Bags, bottles belongings

are thrown to the reeds.
The heron takes flight.

The Desire of the City in a Canal Bank Walk

after Paddy Kavanagh

Consider the nature of the city
leafy with love Grand Canal banks, between
traffic jammed roads where cars beep, cycle brakes scream
and Georgian terraces reign with dignity.
It's a vast repository of time
the couple kissing on an old seat
where later you will sit and we will meet
the dead: girl, poet, bench bound man, shadow this rhyme.

The discarded days of some who've walked here
while others lives are marked by monuments of stone
drinkers, walkers, tenters, loners, dreamers
the ones who sin and the ones who atone.
Let these irises see those who come near
memories bound in mud and words persevere.

Elemental

You come to me, a kaleidoscope of images
formed by the eye of the camera, viewed
through the lens of my desire. Of the earth,
you come in mayshine by the canal, warm
dampness beneath fresh leaves. We follow
the water until I have to turn back but later
the water pulls us together. I feel your body
beneath my fingers, your hard curves,
your thick hair. After many months of grasping air,
you are here between my hands, solid.
And I become real. The flints of desire, sharp
and shining make fire as they have for millenia.
Image, captured light, now released, keeps all things free.
The tones of air on chords are all I have.
The resonance of sound within my ear tapping
bones together to make a music all its own.

Vitrified

It gleams in the museum showcase.
An interesting specimen found in the canal
on dredging day. It was wedged
between a shopping trolley and a suitcase.
All of these items are displayed in the gallery.
A carefully curated project: women in 21st century Dublin.
What can we learn from trolleys, glass hearts and suitcases?

Inside the display case, there's a glass heart.
Inside the heart there's grit
which entered through the open tubes.
The heart is so life-like it allows
the flow of air and particles. Looking in
I hear the sound it would make if I shook it
the rattle of stones in glass.

Over time it fills with soil and a seed
finds its way in, begins to grow
nourishing itself. It shoots its stem
through the tubes. The roots reach down
touch the glass edges of the heart.
It becomes a vessel for another life.

One day the roots push too hard
against the edges of the heart,
the stem grows too wide.
The heart is shattered into fragments
each one reflecting the larger world.

I am Chaos

I am Kayos
The scattering of bones
the ashes of burned bones
light, riding the wind
visible in a ray of sun
on a low winter's day
Those particles are me
you breathe me in
I touch your alveoli
you exhale
with a cough

I am Kay Os
Without bounds, I flourish
I move from place to place
cross river and mountain and sea
desert tundra I am made to travel
dressed in flesh, fed by blood
I pump myself 'round the world
circulate oxygen to all organs
keep you alive
movement is life
stillness is kin to death

I am Kaios
I am not.
Vast emptiness is all I offer
no answers only questions
silence
darkness
no mindfulness here
empty mind, no mind
the great devouring
all of us eaten alive
only gnawed bones remain
sun bleaches
wind borne sand powders

I am Kay O's
entrusted who I am to o
the circle of life
the ring around me
large enough to be forgotten
small enough to hold me together

Differential Calculus for Lovers

i
To deliver you from the preliminary terrors

I've known this man a number of weeks
his dealings have been straight and clear
his online photos are of him, he buys
the drinks, listens well, remembers.

In the flesh he's firm, smells good
he'll dress to suit your style
instruments are his language, tunes them well
people too, they tell him why a bar has such a name

where the hostel in that book would be
and he follows pointed finger out the road.
He has rescued art from rubbish skips
the painting hangs in the home he shares.

He forgets to send the photo, lures women
through the looking glass to hobbit beds.

ii
Please note: in all exercises dealing with curves, students will find it extremely
instructive to verify the deductions obtained by actually plotting the curves.

Women in glass houses should sext with care;
keep clothes and caution close to hand.

iii
Maxima and Minima

A quantity which varies continuously is said to pass by or through a maximum or minimum value when in the course of its variation the immediately preceding values are both smaller or greater respectively, than the value referred to. An infinitely great value is therefore not a maximum value.

A lover who vacillates is best allowed to pass by. If, preceding meetings, texts are greater in number and length than post meetings or if messages come in uncomfortable clusters followed by wordlessness, he is bottom of the barrel and not top of the range material.

On a ship there are two barrels
one full of frogs from this country
and one full of frogs from that country.
Only one barrel is covered.
Curious, she asks, 'Why?'

'Because in this country when a frog
tries to escape the other frogs pull
her back in. In that country however
they climb on top of each other and escape.'

iv

We classify all quantities into two classes: constants and variables.

In calculus we are dealing with rates of growth.

What effect on the process of differentiating is caused by the presence of constants?

Skin is the largest organ, plays pleasure through the body
when tuned in the right hands. Skin is an organ of delight
spread all over, holding nerves poised for joy wanting
only to be touched. Skin is an organ, so close to orgasm
waiting for fingertips to touch where desire spills
from the pores, each cell a symphony
whose rhythm comes from deep inside.

v

On true compound interest and the law of organic growth

Your hard sell
has forced my hand.
I have paid the price
which you demand.

vi

On different degrees of smallness

∫dx, the sum of all the little bits of x

Do many minutes add up to a whole lot?

vii
We may neglect small quantities of the second and third orders therefore
it is best to ensure the room is neither square nor cube.

And prostrate on the bed I lie
this time it's full and wide, note I.
I have my kindle out to read
Anne Carson's poem is what I need.

The Beauty of the Husband is
not a paean to married bliss.
It lists in detail reasons why
women choose to stay with the bad guy.

What tempts a woman to tolerate lies and mental torture?

Dean Swift's portrait observes me,
'hath she a book, what can that be?'
and I quote Anne Carson here,
'why did she hold that scoundrel dear?'

viii
Integrating as the reverse of differentiating

The integral of something is the whole.

What of those who do not wish to integrate?
Who cherish a desire to be separate?

She must collect the pieces, the left-overs
make something of them. There is a beauty
in smallness. Mosaics are not the sum of tiny pieces
they are more; the beauty is brokenness reflecting
light in unpredictable ways.

On the incalculability of differential ratios for unrelated variables

I should have known—a book
on calculus the maths of change
the calculation of relationships
between two variables—did not

bode well nor did Silvanus
slippery god character
who emerged from one culture
adopted by others and twisted

to their meanings. It was
a simple sum from the start.
We are dealing with small quantities
when we vary them we get more.

We vary trying to find the ratio of change
but that is only possible in related variables.

x
Introducing a useful dodge

Sometimes one is stumped by finding that the expression to be differentiated is too complicated to tackle directly.

'Tell all the truth but tell it slant—'
She does not state the angle
of the slant but that at which
the morning light reaches
the pillow where he never slept
is probably the correct figure here.

xi
Geometrical meaning of differentiation

The slope of a curve at a point is however a perfectly defined thing; it is the slope of a very small portion of the curve situated just at that point; and we have seen that this is the same as 'the shape of the tangent to the curve at that point.'

In my dreams love, pleasure,
pain, disgust are perfectly defined.
There are boundaries around them,
no spill, no overflow. In my copybook
the curve is neatly drawn
hangs delicately between

the axes, untouched. In geometry
I learn how slope varies.
Only by pin point focus
can the equation
be written capturing
the exact differential.

The tangent, where it touches,
shares with the curve a ratio
which will, at every other point,
keep them apart.

Spatial Awareness

I turn the map and still I cannot read
it. There is no X which can locate me.
I turn on my GPS. They're telling
me how far I am from there. But where
is there? I face east, you pull me west. Only after
my return you tell me *look up, see where*
they scrape the sky and orient yourself.

My eyes are locked on down, unmoving people:
a mother draws with her child, a sign says
she needs warm clothes; a man sits in a wheel
chair, asleep, his bottle to his side; the gentle
faced veteran who just waits; down by the post
office men who rule whole kingdoms
of waste, work to hold their ground.

I do the crowded High Line side step, step
around. Billboard Einstein watches me
over building sites: *we know more about space*,
the storage company claims. The translator searches
for words which would not take us off the earth
to translate Tranströmer's space. And Hadid
who dreamed space into buildings, created
pokój from a world at war. I put the red map
in the yellow ziploc bag. I know I am lost.

Iveagh Gardens

I am eating sweet cherries, throwing
stones into the flower beds. The roses
have petalled the earth as if a body
has crossed East Coast Road en route
to Besant Nagar cremation ground.

The cherries are juicy. The magpies
gather between rose beds. The pigeons
coo childhood summers to me. Lovers
sit on other benches. They do not kiss.
One rose is still perfect. The bush holds it high.

The cherries shine in my hand. The parents
call their kids back from the rocky hill.
The man calls his dog. The vodka drinker
has taken his argument elsewhere.

I leave some cherries uneaten. I want
to share the joy of juice and sweetness,
this half empty bench, this rose garden
with its petals dying into the soil.

Perishte

This poem has no hero, no heroine
whose cloud breath and ice blink
will bring reason and love to us.

Steam clouds blind us, we are simmering.
Have all the avenging angels perished?
Or are they petrified here in Iveagh Gardens,
reduced to statues beneath crowns of water?

Have the infernal forces emerged
from the hearts of humans, heated flesh
and skin beyond the point of reason?

Whose hand will wave the steam aside
and touch us, remind us of the rituals
of love? There is a time for fire touch,
for ice blink and for earth hug.

We grow from deep, from inferno
through damp earth, to gentle sun
and skywards. When we die
we break down to nourish earth

and in this make warmth. We are watched
over by the clouds, which once were angels.

A long forgotten never quite kiss

Horses' dung is steaming on the cobbles and the red car has brought us to this place,
this courtyard. While I remember the night before, and how, after brushing my teeth,
I had left the bathroom to find him waiting at the door and here we are again,
only a gear stick between us, only horses watching us. Their slow blinking lashes
stroke our every move, and I take in his every move, as we sit in silence
and breathe—I wish his lips on mine but know the engineering of a kiss as intimately
as the mechanics of this car, far simpler to mount a horse and ride without the need
to think, trotting at first over cobbles and later, with the turf beneath our hooves, galloping free.

Deep Topography

i

I step up and through the front door
into your home, spit-smooth neatness
you'd never find in mine,
                                    sink sparkling
as solid silver servant-shone and heat
to warm the soul.
                          The wooden doors
are empire line, neatly dressed in white,
bound beneath breasts in beige silk ribbon.

Deep carpet ripples around couches, Buddha
has the hearth.
                          Upstairs is narrow, I go alone
and find your room; two windows and a space
to breathe.

There's a lock on the door,
                          you did not give me the key.

ii

That night in your bed, I cradled
tears in my arms. I rocked them
to sleep but sorrow needs feeding.

She woke me again and again
demanding my attention, sucking
me dry. You never heard, deep

in your dreams. Morning, you hold
me, calming the ocean
but that was before the storm.

iii

Look closely at my body and you will see the footprints,
                                        boot-marks,
                                        heels,
of all the men who've walked on me. You are soft soled but even then
                                        there are tender places.
                                        Better to crawl than walk,
move forward slowly on hands and knees.

Numbering by Colours

I'm inking colours on your neck and streams of gold
flow from Midas fingers down my spine. I exhale
grey and speak in blue as skin glows green
in your mind's eye, feels purple to your touch.

I'm spelling words upon your back, a cure for curving
relief for pain, the weight of memory lies heavier
here than there. I do not ask the colours of your dreams
the tones of your nightmares, I absorb them through my pores.

The Speed of Light

I think of all the clichés, monstrous cruise ships moving
from the old world to the new, the days of slow travel
across the ocean, from smoky turf fires to cities
made from dreams, buildings stretching to the clouds

and people, so many unknown people, a cliff edge feeling.
Who says the world is not flat when each time
we reach a new place we feel weightless and heavy—
fall through the unknown, subject to a strange gravity.

Cables run deep beneath the Atlantic from Valentia Island
to Heart's Content. Communication between continents
made possible through an oak wood, an ocean and a peaceful
state of mind. On the Blaskets they say, 'God is on the mountain'

on the days when the clouds come down and smother us
in damp silence. Hy-brasil, an island dreamed up by storytellers,
is visible only one day in seven years otherwise hidden in mist.
And a cable, 1600 nautical miles, laid beneath the ocean

connected continents. Now we tap keys, light bounces
through fibres then skywards through the clouds and back
to a small device near Times Square. In the blink of an eye
my lack of lucidity, my ignorance laid bare, no sheet to cover

myself, no word limit to curb intrusion, just clear naked letters.
Light bends in optical fibres, crosses sea through sky but cabled
connection comes through an oak wood, an ocean
and a peaceful state of mind.

And each time it's like the first

planting peas, playing in the mud
dirt under nails, in the palm lines.
I start the work of digging by hand
I am absorbed wholly by the earth
she pulls me in and down. I am full
of concentrating joy, each movement
flows into the next, the mind
is word-silenced, hums in tune
with the soil, the scent enters
my body, damp mould rotting leaves,
perfume peace.

Some morning later I walk barefoot
on cold stone, I notice clematis buds
a pink almost-flower on jasmine,
bulbs piercing the soil, tough rosemary's
delicate blue flower and apple blossom
promising more.

And months later, my feet touch warm tiles
brinjals hide behind leaves, tulsi flowers
despite my presence, malligai gives
generous scented buds, mulliga chaydi
has hot green fruits and bhindi grows
pointing to the sky.

And each time is like the first
to touch mud wherever
to notice the colour and smell
to feel the texture
to know this is what works with me
to make magic, to produce
from pain and dead things
fruit and flower.

Squirrel and the Mother Goddess

i

I am hungry in the cold
it turns me savage
desperate for warmth.
Well-fed, I am kind
put child and elder first
share my kill with the pack.

ii

Squirrel's coat was turning white,
fading red foretold the coming of winter.
As the trees hold the soil, and the soil feeds
the trees on the stone of the mountain;
so the spring births the summer, on the cold
of winter. Squirrel feared white hunger.

iii

I am hunger. I gnaw at you
in quiet times. I nibble the secret
stash, hidden in your memory.
I grow stronger on what you treasure
most, suck your happiness
to the marrow.

iv

Autumn's end and rowan berries fed the hunger
but squirrel's dreams were turning white.
She foraged food to stave off cold,
prepare for the slow sleep of winter.
She searched ash, birch and beech on the mountain;
found nothing to keep for a dead season's feed.

v

I wander in the early autumn mist
in search of nesting grounds
where I can curl.
There I find a rowan tree
heavy with berries
leaves to keep me warm.

I nestle in the early autumn mist
swallow red berries
and sleep.

vi

Squirrel and her young must feed
all through the darkness, keep hunger
away. She has friends on the mountain,
asks blackbird for help. She knows white
is coming and food is required for winter.
Only fattened bodies sleep, survive the cold.

vii

uair éigint
do rachaimid amach
ag siúl
timpeall na boithrín
beidh an lon dubh ag canadh
beimid ag gáire is ag ithe
sméara dúbha
ag deanamh iarracht
labhairt le cheile
í dteanga nua

the tips of our fingers
will be stained purple
my cheeks will be red
from the wind
but the sun will shine
and we will laugh
as the blackbird sings
ag labhairt le teangacha nua
do rachaimid amach
uair éigint

viii

Blackbird knows where sun avoids the cold.
The goddess of the forest, with fruit, feeds
the creatures she loves, all through the winter.
They never forage, no fear of hunger
her gown of rowan red and snowdrop white
makes her beloved mother of the mountain.

ix

We are flying above the Atlantic's raging waves, as they reach
high, send spray to tip our wings. We land on cliffs, search
out precarious nests. Soaring swooping diving rising with
wind-rush energy is our way of life.

x

Squirrel must meet the mother of the mountain,
the goddess who can warm the cold.
Her red is fading, she's almost white.
Oh blackbird, who knows heat and feeds
all through the year, think of my hunger.
Help me demand food for the winter.

xi

The tallum echoes in the emptiness around her and the sound of
many feet slapping the floor in a regular rhythm to the thayum tha
tha thayum thak of the wooden stick. This dark room has incubated
many performances. On the walls only hand prints or oily head
marks are visible. The gods' pictures, she knows, are all confined to
their own room next door, where every inch of wall is covered with
serene-looking gods and goddesses, illuminated by brass dias. The
tools of prayer are kept neatly in the corner—manjal podi in natural
gold and dyed red, oil, cotton wicks and matches. Sandal wood,
vibuthi and a small white lump of camphor are also there beside a
neat pile of well-used prayer books.

xii

Oh squirrel, I will my friend. Before winter
let us go to the heart of the mountain.
The goddess will banish your hunger.
You'll survive full and fat through the cold.
All the small creatures she feeds
have no fear of the season white.

xiii

The colourless woman slipper slaps on steps
key hard in the lock, door opens, fan's switched on.
The world turns, for a moment I fly, blink of her eye,
slap the floor and four feet foot it fast away.

xiv

The goddess gave acorns, an end to hunger and fear
of white winter, seed to an oak, leaves to nourish and protect
mountain soil from the cold, the soil feeds the tree, feeds Squirrel.

xv

Sometimes I feel full
of squirrel love
gathered in times of plenty
wrapped in fear and hoarded
sucked dry in the cold of winter.

The Fox and the Girl

our eyes met
as we both hid
in the undergrowth
he was beautiful
I longed to touch his fur
but held back knowing

he stared still
a nearby twig crack
startled him— I watched
as he fled downhill
until he disappeared
beneath the brow

to reappear at night
while I slept

that summer I learned to scheme
I knew he would not come to me
if I seemed needy of his presence
I crept around—well hidden
left bits here and there
and waited

patience was my lesson
I learned it well

Wood Lover

i

kissing's out of fashion when the gorse is out of bloom
I am furze, grow where soil
is less and wind is more. Shallow
but hardy I withstand storms,
burn fast and hot, warm your home.
I do not settle there
mountainside lover me
wild goat, feral and free.

ii

poison yew with berries
so red and soft
the flesh is tempting
but the seed is poison

mediaeval
love flower
refused me scent
you excuse it, but we know
refused me
love
mediaeval

rowan, red-berried
protective tree
survives harsh soil
root of woman and rune

iii

yew admire the plot of five
I know nothing of them
the lone tree is mine

57

iv

Your eyes can see beneath the bark
follow the grain, guess the texture.
Each beam, each rafter, each latch
and brace you imagined into its place.
A testament to the power of your dreams,
skill of your hands, strength of your desire
to make visible what you see in wood.
You saw my shadow in a block of ash.
I want to make a poem for you.
I know some words but do not know
enough to form an object of beauty
from this clog of desire your eyes can see
beneath the bark.

v

my lover was a yew tree
and I became a mountain ash

my lover was a man of wood
and I became a woman of glass

my lover was a man of song
and I became a woman of words

my lover was a maker of mazes
and I became a solver of puzzles

my lover became a happy man
and I knew my work was done

vi

In a Japanese tea house, a flame heats water. A hand lifts the
pan and pours the water onto tea leaves. The first round is
discarded, the second left to brew. The sisal matting leaves its
mark on skin. The only sounds are soft: breathing, steaming,
pouring and the shiver of summer leaves in this space
suspended above the rootfull soil, beneath a baked clay roof.
The side doors slide back, allowing in leaf strained light.

the smell of charcoal
in a damp forest, the taste
of tea on your tongue

quiet scent of you
hidden place of us, breathing
me in, releasing

make your body a boat

your ribs provide the frame
your skin keeps me warm and dry
inside my craft I travel
over waves across seas

shaken and tossed I feel alive
protected by your bones
fleshed out with care
I feel your strength around me

let me breathe you in through my skin
until boat and body become one
tossed to and fro in the wildness of water
rising and falling with the breath of the ocean

Kattumaram

I want to write you
            a poem of wood and water,
the forest and the sea. I stare
            into Dun Laoghaire harbour,
luminous blue air, tinkle
            of boats on waves
all wood and water, sun
            on sea, gold and blue.

Then I see them
            in the Bay of Bengal.
They stand on water, shadows
            of men so far away. Generations
have found whispering trees
            to strip and bind.
On these they search for fish.
            Life and limb on logs,

and I am here with you,
            painting their image in words,
how wood and water meet
            in the miracle of catamaran.
You dream of travel,
            rooted in your forest.

Red Apples

i

I hold the corer
to the apple
dig it in deep
it bleeds red
onto the white board.
A pool gathers
I regret.

ii

Don't reply until I—
enjoy until—raw—meat.
Take it all off,
if you can, helps render
the fat visible.
A tidy work-space is essential.
Fry the entire thing
fat side down.
It is important to enjoy yourself.
You don't need any oil
for that. Have everything
prepped. Peel the skin off.
Be proud of your work.
Seed this area with salt.
It will get messy, piss blood
everywhere. If you can,
keep it simple.
A knife too blunt will fail.

iii

It is August and we are luminous. We have stored the warmth and sunshine of summer in our bodies, the radiant nectar of long bee filled days, hours droning by canal banks. The heron has plumped up and paired. I have unbolted darksome desire. The simple love of Maghnoon is not my song. I love in jazz, improvised around the melody of hunger and loss. My body quickens to a symphony of touch. It is August and we must dance for Lúnasa, the love of loss, the loss of love, as the summer sun fades into the winter moon.

iv
my body is clay dug from the river
moulded by hands on the plinth
spinning spinning
so fast I cannot think
legs work to keep the wheel turning
hands knead my body
until I am formed in the shape of desire

v
I am curled inside myself
nothing above or below

a tendency to devastation
the habit of sadness

experience teaches me the
inequality of happiness

no revolutionary ideals
just a child's why?

vi

I want to take the ripe words,
toss them in an oak barrel,
then barefoot dance to their tune,
until my sweat and joy mix salty sweet
into the juice. Here I need to add something
to ferment the wine or maybe, like Jesus,
with spells I can make magic.

vii

I'm sitting in the sun
red warmth behind my lids
cool blue-eyed you
at a safe distance

drinking tea, on a red rug
cold of iron bench pushing through
you the length of a long breath
away from me

eating oranges, we
are in a locked garden,
I hold the key, you hold
me here

viii

From each one something
from me everything

the force keeps me moving
head-spinning body turning

I am not bounded
I am not infinity

I am faded shirt
I am worn denims

order is a distant dream
chaos my moving current

I am chapped heels, split ends
I am dry skinned and callous

ix

The winter moon, fades into no-moon, days peeled
from the circumference of light, from circle to crescent
to darkness. The warmth of darkness, a place I can be
safe and invisible, that space behind my eyes where I am
alone. Red, the colour of lipstick and blood and sex. Yes,
sex is red, as desire is blue, a blue note always humming
behind the melody. The flame is hottest where it's blue.

x

This time I gently shook the branches
collected only apples which fell
into my hands. Patience is an art
form, the skill of choosing
one moment from all eternity.

Eorann's Song

I'm left with your crimson cloak
your silver clasp lies warm in my hand
as you bolt in anger
dragged away by your rage

your love-space, never cold
is warmed by another
but it's you I desire
in the bright light of day

when your mind split
you rent us asunder
I staggered, you flapped
you flew away

you dream strange migrations
on narrow paths
sheer cliffs
high in thin air

as I watch you rise
your hair turns to feather
my skin feels plucked
you soar far above

I am left with your empty cloak
your silver clasp lies cold in my hand
I'm rent asunder by your bolt of anger
love drowned in the storm of your rage

I am Penelope

endless suits come
they desire my wealth and power
they sit in waiting knots

by day I weave these words
letters to my lover
who is alive, I know

I know because we meet
by night we unravel
the work of day

we tear asunder
carefully constructed texts
we pull poems apart

searching for the truth
which will release us
from our nightmares

free us to be creatures of the day
strolling holding hands
I grip my pen

I spread black ink
on the bright paper
darkness lurks behind each phrase

every word is shadowed
my body bent over the page
entangled in the lines

fear fettered
I feel you
pin me down
force me open

I don't know women at all.
Or that side of many of them.

after Anne Carson

Women in the off hours
measuring time, splicing infinity
into exquisite instruments of torture.

I remember asking why it is 'sweet sixteen'
and my father fumbling for a reply.
There is no good answer when you're caught

red-handed, making a fist of it
cut off and flying across seas
to claim new bodies, new lands with blood.

'Shame is a rusty edge' used to remove—
the lid of a tin can wielded by
the old woman, cutting device, before

it grows to hang between my legs
sharp shrill pain pierces me
I bleed.

That side is inside.
Without contortion or mirror
I cannot see myself.
Besides what use is knowing
how scar tissue looks
when you've grown it cell by cell.

Marvell's Garden and Me

i

How vainly men themselves amaze
To win the palm, the oak, or bays,
And their uncessant labours see
Crown'd from some single herb or tree,

ii

We walk in circles. You open
with the story of a sadness
months back. The dogs have raced
their shadows, chased their breaths
up and down the grass. The children climb
the evergreen oak and practice
jumping from its heights and you
and I, we just look on. We walk
in circles trying to divine, we walk
searching for what flows beneath
the city's stones, our words.

iii

Thursday finds me tightrope walking on telephone wires and in
the age of mobile phones the wireless rules. I must not look
down or pause to consider. Keep my eyes peeled to the screen.

So much we do blind, by sense of touch. So much we know by
sense of smell.

iv

Evergreen oak, eternally condemned,
allowed itself be used for the cross of Christ.
Banished from homes, unforgiven to this day.

v

Meanwhile the mind, from pleasure less,
Withdraws into its happiness;
The mind, that ocean where each kind
Does straight its own resemblance find,
Yet it creates, transcending these,
Far other worlds, and other seas;
Annihilating all that's made
To a green thought in a green shade.

vi

We walk in circles
trying to divine.
Circle each other,
trying to decide.
Side by side observe
our dogs and kids.
Dogged by the past
we play hide and share.
We pass each other
on the street
and then retreat.

vii

We bisect our round, divide the time
we spend, the narratives we spin
with loops weaving in and out to check
on kids and dogs, and answer calls.
We cut ourselves in two
and you take half and half I do.

viii

Each year the boy in holly, girl in ivy, dance to bring
fertility back after the winter. Holly's leaves act as
lightning conductors. In case of storm, stand here.

ix

Here at the fountain's sliding foot,
Or at some fruit tree's mossy root,
Casting the body's vest aside,
My soul into the boughs does glide;

x

Our dance of circles has us moving backwards
towards the future, describing loop on loop.

xi

If every path we walk's a line and yours
and mine are strong enough to catch the light
and hold the drops, from home to park and park
to home and home to shops and back,
between canal and road and street and square,
these routes which form the boundary, would we
find beneath entangled lives moments which glow
in the darkness, a way to be free of time.

xii

A laurel leaf rubbed on a doorstep keeps away
unwanted visitors, broken in half by lovers it
becomes a promise to meet again.

xiii

Fond lovers, cruel as their flame,
Cut in these trees their mistress' name;
Little, alas, they know or heed
How far these beauties hers exceed!
Fair trees! wheres'e'er your barks I wound,
No name shall but your own be found.

xiv

These are the fruits of our garden time
we have not carved names on bark
but tapped to screen, delivered
read, the trick is to tap so lightly
no blood is drawn.

          A mark is made one needle
at a time. We wonder will the tattoo take,
will we still like the look in months
to come, or seek lasers to remove
all trace of colour, leave only a faint scar.

xv

```
An atomic orbital is a mathematical function that
describes the wave-like behavior of either one
electron or a pair of electrons in an atom. This
function can be used to calculate the probability
of finding any electron of an atom in any
specific region around the atom's nucleus.
```

xvi

To write upon a piece of beech is spelling in an ancient
way as Ogham did. Beech, bok, Buche, book.

xvii

When we have run our passion's heat,
Love hither makes his best retreat.
The gods, that mortal beauty chase,
Still in a tree did end their race:

xviii

I watch you leave
arm around your child
the circle complete.

xix

We carry our wireless
devices emitting signals
leaving a trail, marking
our route magnetically.
We move attracted
and repelled in unsteady
orbits—as yet there's no
equation to explain
the new planetary arrangement,
undiscovered stars
or maybe moons,
not yet defined.

Could be an asteroid on a path
of destruction hurtling towards me.
It is early and still dark.
There's a chance it's just a shooting star,
about to disappear before it's ever fully known.

xx

When you carry a spark the world becomes kindling.

xxi

I sit on cold rock
but still I'm burning—
An unnoticed ember
has become a small flame
I should shut off the air
smother it
before I am ash.

Ash, rowan, ruby berries
fruit of fairies,
magical, intoxicating,
poisonous, protecting.

Burning tree
speak to me.

From Science to Sex in Six Easy Steps

The taxonomy of Linnaeus
like the rest of us
has its origins in sex,
or sexual organs at least—
from the massive poescopia grey
(cunthead or pisspot whale)
to the tiny labia minor earwig
the clearly rather sexy bear
ursus fornicatus magnus
to the overexcited scientific reaction
to a shell: volva volva volva
Freud would have enjoyed
interviewing the person who named
a mollusc peniscillus penis
and an orchid orchis mascula.

But let's face it, Georgia O'Keefe
painted flowers rich and textured
we could recognise as parts of us
perhaps more clearly than our own
vaginas in a line up…cunts in a call out,
quims in a queue. Imagine the man
who would not know his own to see
but we? We know by touch, by feel
but sight?

And my friend tickled her courgette flower
with stamens when the bees were few
that year the courgettes grew, as big
as big as babies.

The truth 'slant ways' is barely visible
unless you are shown—we rarely show—
and even then, with legs apart you peer
up close so near, unless you promise
pleasure, incite the clit, you will not see it
in all its glittering glory.

A long time ago down there on Grafton St.
they asked me to read aloud a masturbation how-to
for radio, a step by step how to pleasure yourself
but then I felt too shy, suggested someone
else. Now I hope others do not need a guide
and know that their pleasure,
however, they do not need to hide.

I have an offer of a fabric fanny, made up
of all my threadbare shirts to expose the material
of my life, the centre of my universe a hole, a space,
a crack from which so much has come and into
the joys of which I have fallen many times
yes yes yes.

I shall hang this pouch of pleasure on my wall
I am a shameless hussy, I celebrate my pussy.

Gymnosophists

gliding naked into the warm
water, bodies already oiled,
sliding from the stone edge, bodies
scraped clean, sitting in the warmth,
the grit and grime, the sweat and sludge
of dead cells removed. They sit
suspended in water, lighter
for lack of clothes, for buoyancy
free to float their minds higher,
bodies watered down, doing deals,
exchanging bonds in a fluid way,
man to man.

31 shades of cat madness

my cat
wraps me around his little finger
teaches me flexibility
to stretch my sinews
to pull muscles to their full extent
to open myself up

my cat
plays cat's cradle
swings me, lulls me
to the rhythm of his purrs
his paws leave imprints
runes to be read by others
marks to make me different

my cat
leads me a merry dance
we move in tandem
breathe as one
his eyes are not on me
I follow where I'm led
weighed down by desire
to be relieved of heaviness
to be bled dry
burnt to ashes

my cat
is cock of the walk
I am under his claws
the tread of his paws on my back
soft red scratches
he sketches hieroglyphs on my body
draws pleasure from inside me

my cat
is anybody's,
goes to the highest bidder
I climb spires, towers, mountains
I outbid all comers
but he is never mine

Nawashi and Captive

A Waka

I will let you go
but not till I've made my mark
your loose threads ravel
I want to knot them tightly
suspend you from disbelief

        I will learn the ropes
        keep one foot in the liminal
        eyes fixed on fantasy
        desire wound tight around flesh
        rope: twist of the dream and real

I want you to give
I offer you the sublime
pure exchange, camphor
solid body to pleasure
High Porte, I tax your body

        You may tie me up
        suspend me from star to star
        constellate my body
        every knot constrains us both
        consummation gives freedom

I will tie you down
use loop and coil to fix you
to a single plane
achieve what words cannot
a poem of flesh and blood

        You'll have me utter
        guttural sounds, beyond words
        fine-tuned by your hands
        a tongue of muscle and nerve
        strength to swallow, tasting touch

a knife fetish

you must know
I find blades
beautiful and sharp

knives are dual
a handle to hold
a point to pierce

Old Love Poems Make Me Cry

when I read old love poems
forty, fifty years of solid rock
and children, fossils embedded
in that love, I feel like sand
shifting beneath my daughter's feet

Notes

A LINKISTER PLAYS WITH QUANTUM REALITY – p11
See Amitav Ghosh's *River of Smoke*
Linkister: translator between English, Hindi, Cantonese and Pidgin
Pidgin: meaning business in CPE
Lob, *ishq* and *pyaar* mean love

THE END OF OCTOBER – p12
ii – Quote from anonymous rescuer on Lesvos (edited)
iii – Irish saying: no hearth like your own hearth
iv – Quote from anonymous Syrian person caught between borders.
v – Janina Martinho, on why Jews stayed in Krakow ghetto
vii – A. A. Milne *The House at Pooh Corner*
viii – Dr Seuss *Horton Hears a Who*
xi – Nizar Qabbani, *Footnotes to the Book of the Setback*

RANGER DOMINANCE – p14
After Ethan McCord's testimony to the events of 5th April 2010 in Baghdad.

NUMBERS – p16
Details as recorded in https://www.channel4.com/news/syrias-descent-the-agony-of-aleppos-children.

GHAZAL FOR PARVEENA AND HER SON JAVAID (disappeared 1991) – p17
https://www.inversejournal.com/2020/02/23/where-have-you-hidden-my-new-moon-crescent-by-iffat-fatima/

https://apdpkashmir.com/

TRANSLATED FROM A LIBYAN LIFE IN IRELAND – p20
The following words are transliterated from Arabic:
mojewdia: to be, to exist, existentialism
waheed: alone
Umm Taufiq: mother of Taufiq
fatwa: an opinion
al Ummah: the world wide community of Muslims

MOHN AND MEMORY — p29
Mohn: poppy seed in German
zwishen Sprachen: between languages in German
Es ist Zeit: it is time in German

DIFFERENTIAL CALCULUS FOR LOVERS — p37
Quotes from Edwards, Joseph *Differential Calculus for Beginners*, Macmillan, London 1896

SPATIAL AWARENESS — p43
Pokój means room or peace in Polish.

PERISHTE — p45
Perishte in Urdu and Farsi means angel, possible cognate of perished in English.

THE SPEED OF LIGHT — p50
1858 first cable from Europe to Americas laid from Valentia Island to Heart's Content, Canada.

AND EACH TIME IT'S LIKE THE FIRST — p51
brinjal: aubergine
malligai: jasmine in Tamil
mulliga chaydi: chilli plant in Tamil
bhindi: okra

SQUIRREL AND THE MOUNTAIN GODDESS — p52
vii — Sometime, we will go out walking the roads. The blackbird will be singing and we will be laughing and eating blackberries trying to speak to each other in a new language.

xi —
tallum: rhythm in Tamil
diyas: small lights lit with wicks and oil in earthen pots
manjal podi: turmeric powder in Tamil
vibuthi: ash of cow dung in Tamil

KATTUMARAM — p61

Kattumaram: kattu means to tie and maram is tree. This Tamil compound word gives us the English catamaran.

EORANN'S SONG — p66

Written after reading Seamus Heaney's *Sweeney Astray*. Eorann was Sweeney's wife.

MARVELL'S GARDEN AND ME — p69

Italics are quotes from Andrew Marvell's 'The Garden'.

xv — Quote from LumenLearning.com

Acknowledgements

"Ranger Dominance" first published online at http://wurmimapfel.net/can-can UpStart Blog and in 2021 in *The Disasters of War: An Anthology for Veterans Day,* by Moonstone Arts Centre, Philadelphia.

"Ghazal for Parveena" first published in *a compound of word,* Yoda Press, 2020.

"Iveagh Gardens" first published in *Local Wonders,* Dedalus Press, 2021.

"Old Love Poems Make me Cry" first published online by Dimitra Xidous at https://balckstrongandsweetpoetry.wordpress.com/2013/05/13/fiona-bologer-old-love-poems-make-me-cry/

The poems in this collection are the result of many years of reading, listening, writing, and being heard. Thank you to all those who have inspired me, encouraged me, read me, edited me. A special thank you to the first and second readers of these poems, this manuscript Anne Tannam, Alvy Carragher, Margaret Dee and Moyra Donaldson, Kit Fryatt, Özgeçan Kesici, Srilata K. and Tapasya Narang. To the writing and publishing communities who have welcomed me over the years, Rathmines Writers' Workshop, Airfield Writers, Dublin Writers' Forum, Moonstone Arts Centre (Philadelphia), Poetria (Kerala), A Suitcase of Poetry (online everywhere), Poetry Bus Press, Yoda Press and the Irish Writers' Centre thank you for your support.

A special thank you to Jessie Lendennie and Siobhán Hutson for making these poems sit between these covers. Thank you to Joby Hickey for his photography used on the cover and to Deepthi Govindarajan for her portrait photo.

Fióna Bolger lives with her tall daughter and short dog in Dublin. She has never left Chennai. She is a creative facilitator interested in collaborations and mentoring new voices. She works with Outlandish Theatre Platform and ReWrite. More about her on www.fionabolgerpoetry.com

salmonpoetry

Cliffs of Moher, County Clare, Ireland

"Publishing the finest Irish and international literature."
Michael D. Higgins, President of Ireland